CW01212323

London Borough of Havering
90120000165287

CHILDREN'S
PLANET

Our Oceans

Louise Spilsbury
Illustrated by Khoa Le

W
FRANKLIN WATTS
LONDON•SYDNEY

Franklin Watts
First published in Great Britain in 2024
by Hodder & Stoughton
Copyright © Hodder & Stoughton 2024
All rights reserved

Editor: Julia Bird
Design: Peter Scoulding

HB ISBN 978 1 4451 8625 2
PB ISBN 978 1 4451 8626 9

Franklin Watts, an imprint of
Hachette Children's Group
Part of Hodder and Stoughton
Carmelite House
50 Victoria Embankment
London EC4Y 0DZ

An Hachette UK Company
www.hachette.co.uk
www.hachettechildrens.co.uk

Printed and bound in China

MIX
Paper from responsible sources
FSC® C104740

CHILDREN'S PLANET

Our Oceans

LOUISE SPILSBURY
ILLUSTRATED BY KHOA LE

Oceans are amazing. These huge areas of salty water cover most of our planet. They provide food and homes for all sorts of wonderful wildlife. Tiny ocean plants also make the air that we need to breathe!

Oceans are places for adventure and fun, too. We can swim and surf in the waves. We can build sandcastles, find shells and spot animals at the coast.

Coasts are where oceans meet the land. Here, seaweed clings to rocks to stop the waves from washing it away. Crabs eat the seaweed. Their hard shells protect them from hungry seabirds.

In the water, jellyfish use their tentacles to sting and catch crabs for supper. A sea turtle uses its wide, flat flippers to chase jellyfish to eat. Seals and dolphins dive for fish washed in by the waves.

Coral reefs are full of life. Corals are tiny animals that live in big groups. They build rocky reefs for protection. Algae are like ocean plants. They grow among the coral.

Colourful fish bite off coral and algae with their teeth. Octopuses use their eight arms to grab fish and pop them into their mouth. Giant moray eels dart out of cracks in the reef to snap up octopuses.

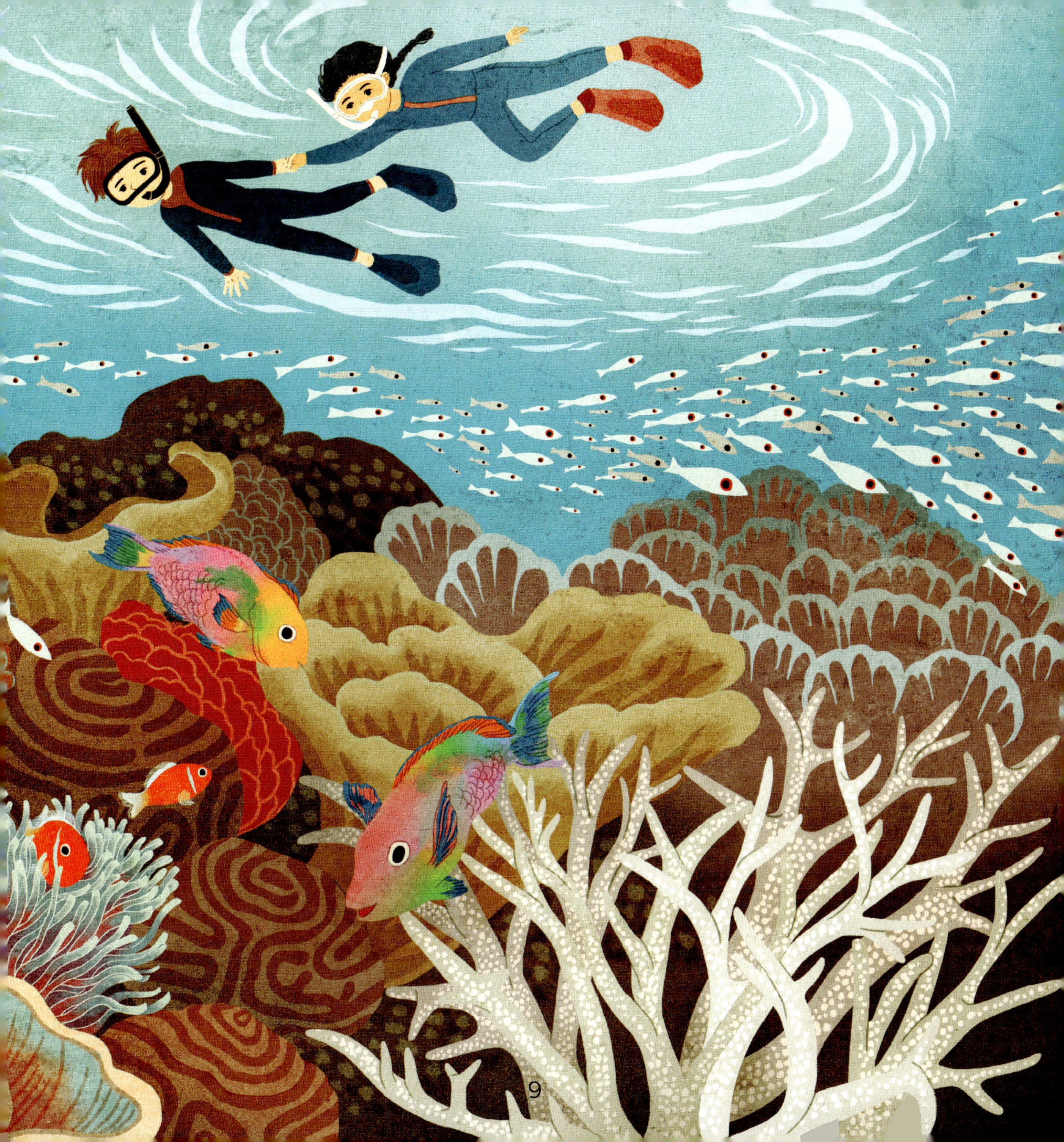

Strange creatures lurk in the deep ocean where it's very cold and dark. One squid has eyes the size of footballs! These capture any available light to help it see.

Some fish use gaping mouths full of needle-sharp teeth to catch dinner. The angler fish dangles a light to lure fish into its jaws.

Some animals have transparent skin to help them hide from danger.

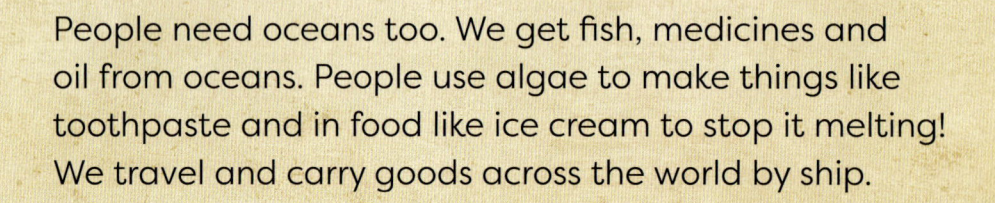

People need oceans too. We get fish, medicines and oil from oceans. People use algae to make things like toothpaste and in food like ice cream to stop it melting! We travel and carry goods across the world by ship.

Oceans also keep our world at a comfortable temperature. The ocean absorbs most of the Sun's heat. Then oceans help to spread the heat evenly around the planet.

13

Oceans help us and our planet a lot. But we're hurting oceans. When people do things like drive cars or heat buildings they burn coal, oil and other fuels. This adds extra gases to the air.

These gases wrap around the Earth. They keep in heat and make our planet warmer. This is called climate change and it is causing some big problems.

Earth's extra heat is melting ice at the Poles. This water flows into the oceans. Some coasts and islands are disappearing underwater as oceans get deeper.
This is bad for coastal animals and us.

Melting ice also harms polar bears. Polar bears hunt seals from floating rafts of ice. When ice rafts melt, polar bears stay on shore. They go hungry and can starve to death.

Oceans are getting too warm. This makes some ocean plants and animals sick. It stops some tiny animals having young. That means less food for animals like fish and seals to eat.

Warmer ocean water also kills the corals that make coral reefs. This robs reef animals of the food and shelter they need to survive. Many fish, turtles and other creatures may disappear.

19

Oceans soak up some of the gases from the air that make our planet warmer. These gases change the water in the oceans. They make it more acidic.

Acidic water stops animals like oysters and mussels from making strong shells. These shellfish cannot survive without tough shells. Fewer shellfish also means less food for other animals to eat.

There are lots of ways we can help oceans. We can reduce the amount of fuel we use to slow climate change. Go on holiday by train instead of plane or car. Ride a kayak instead of a motor boat!

People can also use oceans to reduce fuel use. They can turn the energy in moving water into electricity, instead of using oil and coal to make power.

We can help oceans by keeping them healthy. Waste that goes down drains can flow into streams and rivers and finally into oceans. This can harm ocean life.

That's why we should never flush paints, oils or medicines down sinks and toilets. It's also best to use gentle cleaning products that won't harm ocean life to wash our homes and bodies.

Plastic is a big problem. Sea turtles and other animals swallow plastic waste and can choke on it. They can also get tangled up in plastic nets. Plastic waste in the oceans also releases gases into the air that make Earth warmer.

We can help. We can stop buying plastic stuff that only gets used once. Buy bags, bottles, cups and containers that you can use again and again instead.

Learn all you can about oceans and the amazing animals that live in them. Tell other people why oceans are so important. You could even join a beach clean and help pick up litter.

Visit coasts with friends and family. Being in, on or near the ocean can make us happier and healthier. It also makes people care more about protecting oceans.

29

Glossary

acidic things that contain acid can damage other substances
air a mixture of different gases all around us. The air we breathe contains oxygen which we need to live
climate change changes in the temperatures and weather across the world
flippers wide, flat arms or legs that animals use for swimming
fuel something like coal or oil that can be burned to make energy
gas a substance that is like air and has no fixed shape. Some gases are fuels that can be burned
goods things, such as food or toys, that people can buy
litter rubbish or waste
lure to attract an animal towards somewhere
Poles the North and South Poles, the opposite ends of the Earth
seaweed a plant-like living thing that thrives in oceans
shellfish small creatures that live in water and are protected by a hard shell
tentacles long, bendy animal arms used for grasping, feeling and moving
transparent see-through or clear, like a window

Find Out More

Find the answers to more questions about oceans in
I Wonder Why the Sea Is Salty: And Other Questions about the Oceans,
Anita Ganeri, Kingfisher, 2023

Discover more facts about oceans in
Do You Love Oceans?: Why Oceans are Magnificently Mega!,
Matt Robertson, Bloomsbury Children's Books, 2023

Explore an ocean habitat in
Explore Ecosystems: In an Ocean, Sarah Ridley, Wayland, 2023

Find out more about saving oceans and the planet
It's a Wonderful World: How to Protect the Planet and Change the Future,
Jess French, DK Children, 2022

Things To Do

Look and learn! Take a trip to an aquarium or visit one online on a live webcam or video tour.
Find the facts! Do an ocean animal research project. Pick an ocean animal and find out all you can about it.
Get crafty! Use a paper plate to make a fish bowl. Just cut off the top of the plate and draw brightly coloured fish inside your bowl!
Explore the oceans! Look at a world map to see where the world's oceans are. How many can you find and what are they called?
Make a poster! Cut photos of sea animals from magazines and make a poster about ocean wildlife.
Do an experiment! See how it's easier for things to float in salty seawater! Take two tall glasses of warm water. Add three tablespoons of salt to one glass and stir well until the salt is mixed in. Very gently drop an egg into both glasses of water. What happens?

INDEX

Algae 8, 12
Angler fish 11

Beach cleans 28

Climate change 14-18, 22
Coasts 6
Coral reefs 8, 18
   killing 18
Crabs 6

Deep ocean 10-11
Dolphin 7

Fish 7, 8, 18
Fuels
   coal 23
   oil 23

Jellyfish 7

Moray eels 8

Octopuses 8

Plastic 26-27
   reusable 27
Poles 16
   polar bears 17

Sea turtles 7, 18
Seabirds 6
Seals 7
Seaweed 6
Shells 5
Shellfish 21
Squid 10

Warming seas 18-19
Waste 24-27